12 THINGS TO KNOW ABOUT THE IRON AGE

by Meg Marquardt

12 STORY LIBRARY
MORE TO EXPLORE

www.12StoryLibrary.com

12-Story Library is an imprint of Bookstaves.

Photographs ©: Portable Antiquities Scheme/CC2.0, cover, 1; Paolo Trovo/Shutterstock.com, 4; Stylone/Shutterstock.com, 5; Fokin Oleg/Shutterstock.com, 6; PD, 7; PD, 8; Allison Laing/PD, 9; Sanjar Alimov/CC4.0, 10; jsp/Shutterstock.com, 11; PD, 12; PD, 13; Anastasios71/Shutterstock.com, 14; John Steeple Davis/PD, 15; Mehrdad Jamali firouzabadi/CC4.0, 16-17; Steve Swayne/CC2.0, 17; Classical Numismatic Group, Inc./CC3.0, 17; dpa/Alamy, 18; Rosemania/CC2.0, 19; Classical Numismatic Group, Inc./CC3.0, 20; Berthold Werner/CC3.0, 21; Cleveland Museum of Art/Gift of the John Huntington Art and Polytechnic Trust/CC1.0, 21; Nick Taylor/CC2.0, 22; Masoudkhalife/CC4.0, 23; User:Colin/CC4.0, 24; gabriel12/Shutterstock.com, 25; Sven Rosborn/PD, 25; Walaa/CC3.0, 26; Maarten van Heemskerck/PD, 26; Wellcome Images/CC4.0, 27; Åge Hojem, NTNU Vitenskapsmuseet/CC2.0, 28-29

ISBN
9781632357687 (hardcover)
9781632358776 (paperback)
9781645820499 (ebook)

Library of Congress Control Number: 2019938630

Printed in the United States of America
July 2019

About the Cover

A hoard of Iron Age coins discovered in England.

Access free, up-to-date content on this topic plus a full digital version of this book. Scan the QR code on page 31 or use your school's login at 12StoryLibrary.com.

Table of Contents

1 The Iron Age Started and Ended at Different Times

Ruins of a stone fort in northern Europe dating from the Iron Age.

The Iron Age started at different times in different places. It also ended at really different times. In northern Europe, the Iron Age started around 450 BCE (Before the Common Era). It ended around 800 CE (Common Era). That is over 1,200 years of the Iron Age.

By contrast, in Greece, the Iron Age started in 1100 BCE. It ended around 510 BCE. This means Greece was in and out of the Iron Age before it even started in northern Europe.

The different start times have to do when people began working with iron. Metalsmiths made tools and weapons out of iron. The different end times are more complicated. Sometimes a new civilization arose and conquered other civilizations. For example, the Roman Empire caused the Iron Age to end in most of Europe. The Romans brought new ideas, technologies, and social systems. They established new settlements and ways of doing things. The Iron Age was left behind.

The Iron Age was full of its own empires. These included the Persian and Celtic empires. They built great palaces and invented new religions. The Iron Age is the last great prehistoric age.

3,400
Years ago when iron was first used

- The people of the Hittite empire were the first to use iron.
- The Hittites lived in what is now Turkey and Syria.
- They were technically a Bronze Age civilization. Their use of iron means they were ahead of almost every other Bronze Age civilization.

Hattusa was the capital of the Hittite Empire. Its ruins were added to the UNESCO World Heritage list in 1986.

2

Iron Was the New Metal of Choice

Iron is a strong metal. It is great for making weapons and tools. However, it took humans a while to figure out how to use it. First, they had to find iron ore. Ore is a raw version of a metal. It's found in the ground. There's plenty of iron ore all over the earth.

The next step is tricky, though. Iron has to be smelted. Smelting happens when an ore is heated. It has to be heated to a high temperature to get the metal out. Once iron is out of the ore, metalworking can begin.

Before iron, people mostly worked with copper and bronze. These metals melt at a lower temperature. People would pour them into molds. As the metals cooled and hardened, they took the shape of the mold. That's how bronze swords and armor were made.

Iron melts at a higher temperature. Instead of cooling in molds, it is worked by smiths. Think back on scenes from movies about knights. The smiths in those movies heat

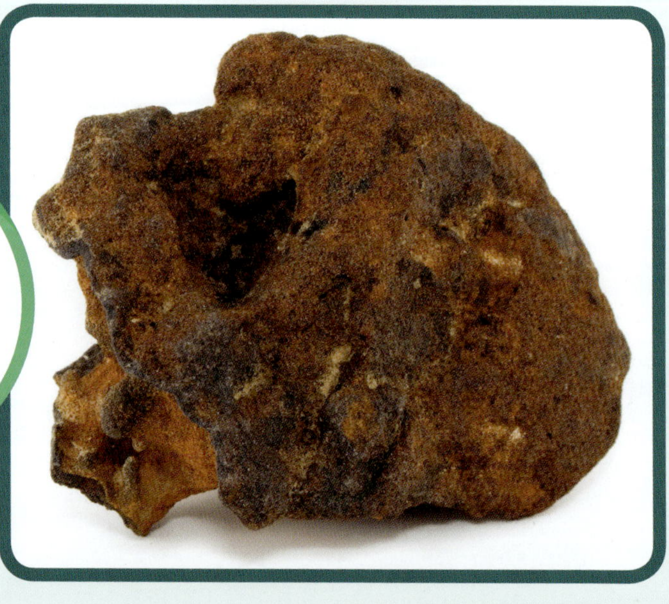

A chunk of iron ore after it's been mined from the ground.

19

Number of iron objects found in King Tut's tomb

- King Tut (short for Tutankhamun) was a ruler of ancient Egypt. He lived before the Iron Age.
- In his tomb, researchers found an iron dagger and iron beads.
- They discovered the iron had come from a meteorite. People used this iron before they discovered iron ore and learned how to smelt it.

Tutankhamun's iron dagger and gold sheath were discovered next to his body.

metal, then use a hammer to pound out a shape, like a sword. That is how iron is worked. Iron is also much cheaper than bronze.

IRON AGE AFRICA

Ancient Egypt was a famous empire in the northeast corner of Africa. What about the rest of the continent? During the Iron Age, much of Africa was nomadic tribes. But some civilizations worked with iron. These included people in other areas of Africa, such as Nigeria. They made iron spears and knives. The rest of Africa was working with iron by 1600 CE.

3 Iron Tools Made Life Easier

The Iron Age was a time of new technology. New technology meant better farming. Today, when we think of technology, we picture smartphones and computers. But those are just tools we use to lead a more efficient life. That's what technology has always been. The innovations of the Iron Age may look low-tech, but at the time, they were brilliant new inventions.

One example is the plow. Plows have sharp metal blades. These blades break up the ground as the plow is dragged along. Before the plow came along, people used sticks or hoes. They did the work by hand. By the Iron Age, plows were being drawn by horses or cattle. This was a huge change.

Celtic people used a complex plow. It had two parts. In the front was a sharp blade. This blade broke up the earth. On the back was a series of smaller blades. These blades smoothed out the earth. They also dug neat rows. This allowed farmers to plant their crops evenly. This type

The 13 surgical instruments found in a grave.

of farming is called arable farming. Using horses and plows cut down on the time it took to get the land ready for planting.

FIRST USE OF FERTILIZER

For a long time, researchers thought fertilizers were first used in the Iron Age. For example, the Celts used fertilizers made of trees, sand, and soil. However, new research in 2013 showed that people had been using fertilizers for much longer. The use of manure as a fertilizer started 8,000 years ago. That's all the way back in the Neolithic Age.

13

Surgical instruments found in a grave in Stanway, Essex, England

- The grave where they were found is called the Doctor's Grave. It dates from around the Roman conquest in the year 43 CE.
- The instruments included forceps, needles, scalpels, and a surgical saw.
- An ancient board game was also found in the grave.

4 The Iron Age Was a Time of Constant War

This stone relief of the Assyrian Army in battle dates from 865 BCE.

The Iron Age was a time of empires. Wars were fought over land and resources. With so many battles being fought, the nature of warfare changed. During the Iron Age, many modern fighting techniques were introduced.

One new thing was conscription. Conscription is when a government forces someone to join the army and fight. A modern example is the draft, where people are randomly selected to serve. In the United States, a draft is only used during a time of war. In ancient times, conscription looked a little different.

Ancient conscription created standing armies at all times. A standing army is a permanent army. The empire didn't need to be at war. Conscripts were paid a wage. They helped the empire patrol conquered territories that were far away.

Conscription usually only lasted a few years. But some conscripts might choose to serve for life. The

120,000-150,000

Number of people in the Iron Age Assyrian Army

- The Assyrian Army was a fighting force in the Middle East.
- As many as 50,000 men might fight in a single battle.
- In the Bronze Age, the largest armies were only around 5,400 men.

INVENTING WEAPONS

The Iron Age saw many new weapons. Swords were bigger and stronger. Swords and knives were made specifically for fighting on horseback or on chariots. The Iron Age was the last great boom in making weapons for a long time. Three thousand years later, gunpowder would be discovered. After gunpowder, a whole new arsenal of weapons was created.

Iron Age was the start of military service becoming a profession. Someone had to make sure the army kept running, even as conscripts came and went. A standing army was only as strong as its leaders.

Assyrian warriors were well-equipped for battle.

5 Greece Went Dark

Before the Iron Age, there was the Bronze Age. The Mycenaean civilization was a great Bronze Age civilization in the south of Greece. At the end of the Bronze Age the culture suddenly collapsed. No one knows why. There might have been an earthquake or an invasion.

When a great civilization collapses, it leaves a hole. Thriving cities fall and people have to scratch out a living in towns or villages. The first part of the Iron Age in Greece was known as a Dark Age. While other places were busy making new weapons and new forms of government, Greece was struggling. There had once been grand palaces, but now people lived small. They left the cities for settlements that could be easily defended.

This doesn't mean that nothing happened in Greece. The people learned how to work with iron. Someone else likely taught them. They were still involved with trade and contact with other civilizations. The Greek Dark Age lasted for about 400 years. But the Greeks bounced back, creating new types of art and new ways of writing.

Some believe an invasion by the Sea Peoples caused the start of the Dark Age.

776 BCE

Year of the first Olympic Games

- This first Games mark the end of the Greek Dark Ages.
- A foot race was the only athletic event.
- Runners sprinted in a short race of 629 feet (129 m).

WERE DARK AGES REALLY THAT DARK?

Greece wasn't the only part of the world to have a Dark Age. Much later, Europe also went through a Dark Age. However, people disagree about the use of that term. Some think "Dark Age" implies that no progress was being made. But maybe archaeologists just don't know a lot about the time period. In reality, a lot might have been happening in the Dark Ages. Researchers will have to keep working to find out.

Lists of Olympic victors were recorded on papyrus.

6

New Forms of Government Started Up

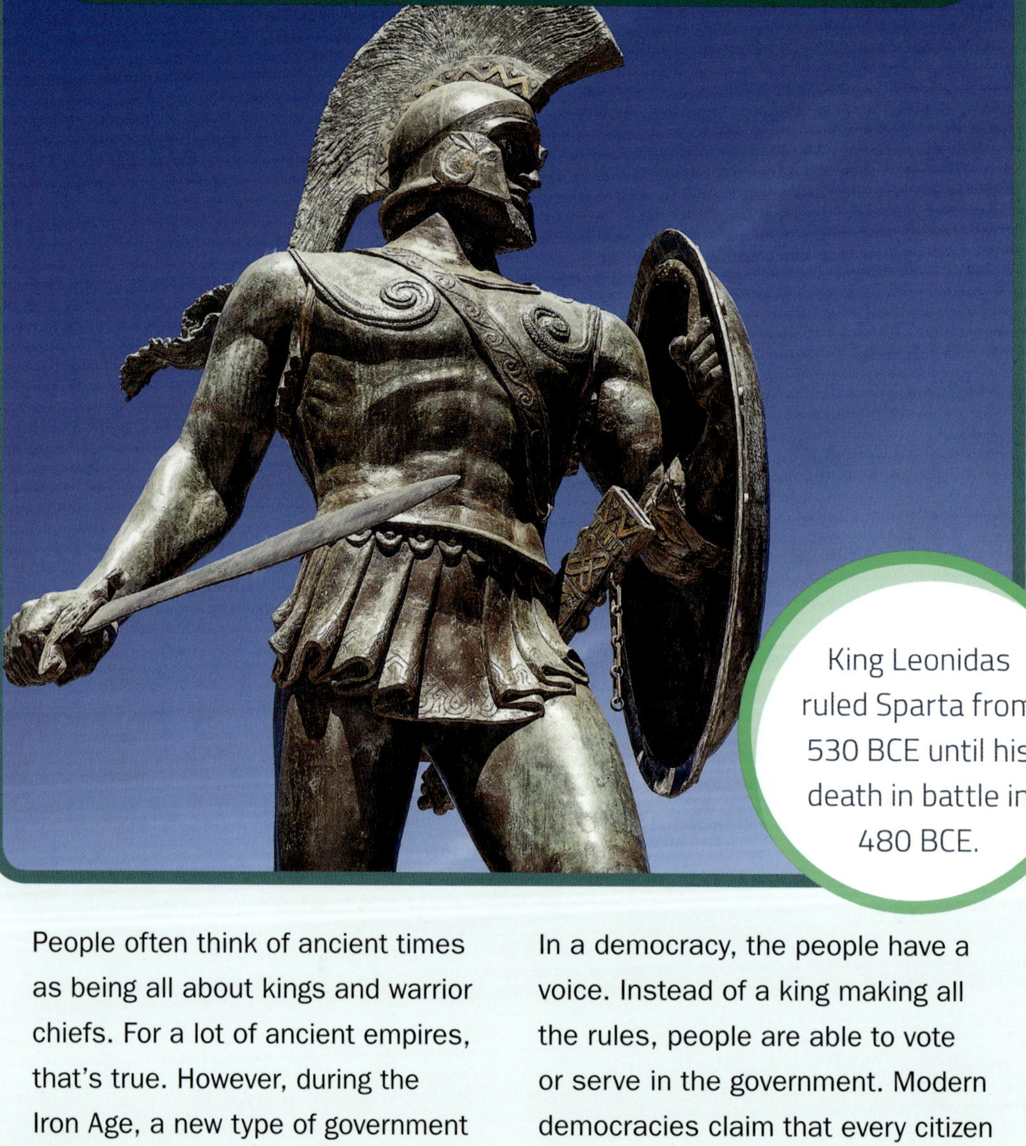

King Leonidas ruled Sparta from 530 BCE until his death in battle in 480 BCE.

People often think of ancient times as being all about kings and warrior chiefs. For a lot of ancient empires, that's true. However, during the Iron Age, a new type of government started to take shape. This government was a very early form of democracy.

In a democracy, the people have a voice. Instead of a king making all the rules, people are able to vote or serve in the government. Modern democracies claim that every citizen is able to vote and run for office. In ancient times, democracy looked different.

Sparta grew to become a dominant military power.

For example, the Greeks invented a system called the *polis*. In Greek, the word "polis" means "city." It can also mean the people who live in the city. A king who ruled a city also ruled its people. In a polis, the king would think about his people when making decisions. This gave the people more of a voice. They could reach out to their ruler and make their needs known.

This wasn't exactly democracy. People couldn't vote. They just had to hope their ruler would think about their needs. However, the polis laid the groundwork for democracy to start right around the corner.

1,000

Polies in ancient Greece

- Polies were large cities, often with fortification against invaders.
- Athens, Sparta, and Rhodes were polies.
- Sparta was the biggest, at 3,200 square miles (8,288 square kilometers).

DEMOCRACY FOR WHOM?

The polis didn't treat everyone equally. In fact, only free men had political rights. Women and slaves did not have rights. Neither did foreigners. In any given city, only 10 percent of the population was a member of the political polis. Today, a democracy usually promises political protection to all of its citizens.

7 Architecture Became More Complex

In the Middle East during the Iron Age, beautiful buildings rose up. One important discovery was Hasanlu Tepe in northwestern Iran. This large archaeological site contains many remains of buildings. Some had spiral staircases. Instead of going straight, they twist and turn. Such a design creates an elegant sight in a building.

Some large structures in Hasanlu needed supports. For these, ancient architects designed buttresses. Buttresses stick out from a wall and help keep it stable.

In Hasanlu, buttresses are used on entrances to temples and courtyards. They mark certain areas of the city as important.

Great architecture was also happening outside the Middle East. One of the most famous surviving buildings is the Parthenon. It was designed by two architects named Ictinus and Callicrates. The Parthenon was built in Athens about 2,500 years ago. It is 228 feet (69.5 m) long. It has 69 huge columns. Each column is fluted. Deep valleys are carved into the entire length, from top to bottom.

The archaeological site of Hassanlu Tepe in Iran.

The remains of the Parthenon in Athens, Greece.

It took more than 10 years to build the Parthenon. When it was done, it was a center for worship. The Parthenon was built to honor the goddess Athena, the protector of the city. There once was a giant statue of Athena inside the Parthenon. The statue was lost, but the ruins of the Parthenon can still be visited today.

469

Number of silver talents it cost to build the Parthenon

- A talent was a type of currency.
- A brand-new warship might cost one talent.
- The giant statue of Athena was covered in gold. It cost 1,000 talents.

THINK ABOUT IT

If you had the chance to build a great structure, what would you build and why?

8

New Religions Formed

A lot of new religions formed during the Iron Age. One was the religion of the Scythians. The Scythians were a nomadic people in the Middle East. Their religion involved animal sacrifice. They also mummified their dead. Mummification keeps dead bodies from decaying. The Scythians would bury their mummified dead with a sacrificed horse. They believed the horse would accompany the dead person into the afterlife.

Another new religion was that of the ancient Celts. Their empire stretched from the United Kingdom through most of northern and central Europe. Because their empire was so large, they left a lot of artifacts archaeologists can study. From these artifacts, researchers know that the Celts practiced polytheism. This means they believed in more than one god or goddess.

The religion of the Celts is a good example of how ideas can spread and change. Ancient reports show the Celtic gods had slightly different names in different places. In one area, a god might be called Lleu. In another, he might be called Lugh.

Tattoos are still visible on this mummified Scythian warrior that dates to 800 BCE.

Celtic goddess Epona was a protector of horses.

BRINGING BACK OLD NORSE BELIEFS

Some people in Denmark, Norway, Sweden, and Iceland are bringing back ancient Norse beliefs and practices. Followers of a new movement called Ásatrú , they worship gods and goddesses from before Christianity. These include Thor, Odin, and Freya. Ásatrú is the fastest-growing religion in Iceland. In 2019, a new Ásatrú temple opened in Iceland's capital city, Reykjavik.

2,000

Number of years ago when Halloween was first celebrated

- Halloween was originally an ancient Celtic festival called Samhain (sow-in).
- The Celts believed the dead returned to the land of the living on October 31.
- In the year 1000 CE, the Catholic church named November 2 All Souls' Day. The church wanted people to celebrate a Christian holiday, not a pagan festival.

9

Money Was Invented

Money didn't always exist. People used to trade for things they wanted or needed. A person who raised cows could trade meat for grain or clothing. By the Iron Age, societies

grew more complex. Trading goods and services didn't always make sense. So a money system was invented.

One advantage of using money is it standardizes purchasing. To standardize something means to make it the same everywhere. Trading isn't standardized. People barter back-and-forth until they reach an agreement. Money helped make the process more fair.

One of the first coins was made in Lydia, an Iron Age kingdom in western Turkey. The coin was a mix of silver and gold. Each coin was weighed so it was the same as every other coin. A lion picture was stamped on one side. Now everyone who had coins could pay the same price for services such as metalworking. This took the guesswork out of the economy.

But another challenge existed. Each kingdom and empire made their own coins. These might be different shapes and sizes. They might be worth more or less. So while coins helped to standardize prices inside an empire, things were still complicated. The economy had room to grow.

A mosaic of Alexander the Great in battle.

91

Number of mints that made coins stamped with Alexander the Great's face

- Mints are places that produce coins and currency.
- Alexander the Great was one of the ancient world's most impressive conquerors. He took over lands from Egypt to India.
- Coins with his face on them were widely used even after he died.

THINK ABOUT IT

If you could design a coin, whose face would you put on it and why?

10

From Small Tribes, an Empire Grew

A relief of the Persian King Xerxes (519-465 BCE) carved into a doorway at Persepolis.

History doesn't progress in the same way everywhere. Some regions move faster than others. Or they move in different directions. By the Iron Age, a lot of societies were living in large cities. However, not all were.

At the beginning of the Iron Age, the Persians were a nomadic people. They moved around the Iranian plateau in the Middle East. Even without great cities, they still had an emperor. Cyrus the Great brought tribes together to make the first Persian Empire in 550 BCE.

The Persian Empire grew to be huge. It stretched from India to Egypt. As it did, it stopped being a nomadic empire. Instead, Persia became a center of art and culture. The people carved intricate patterns into stone. They created beautiful metal jewelry and knickknacks. They were

30

Height in feet (9.1 m) of the tallest wall around Persepolis

- Persepolis was surrounded by three walls to keep out attackers.
- The first was only 7 feet (2.1 m) tall. Behind that was another wall 14 feet (4.3 m) tall.
- These walls are called ramparts. Soldiers and guards walked on the ramparts to watch for trouble.

especially known for weaving rugs. Even today, owning a real Persian rug is considered a sign of wealth.

One of the greatest feats of the Persian Empire was the city of Persepolis. It was founded in 518 BCE. It had a large palace that sat atop terraces. A terrace is a flat surface like a patio. Terraces can be stacked on top of each other to create wide steps. Inside the palace were beautiful brick murals.

Persepolis was conquered in 330 BCE by Alexander the Great. He burned the city to the ground. But the Persians had made remarkable progress from nomadic tribes to a great empire in just 200 years.

The ruins of Persepolis and the terraces it sat atop.

11

Bog Bodies Hold Iron Age Secrets

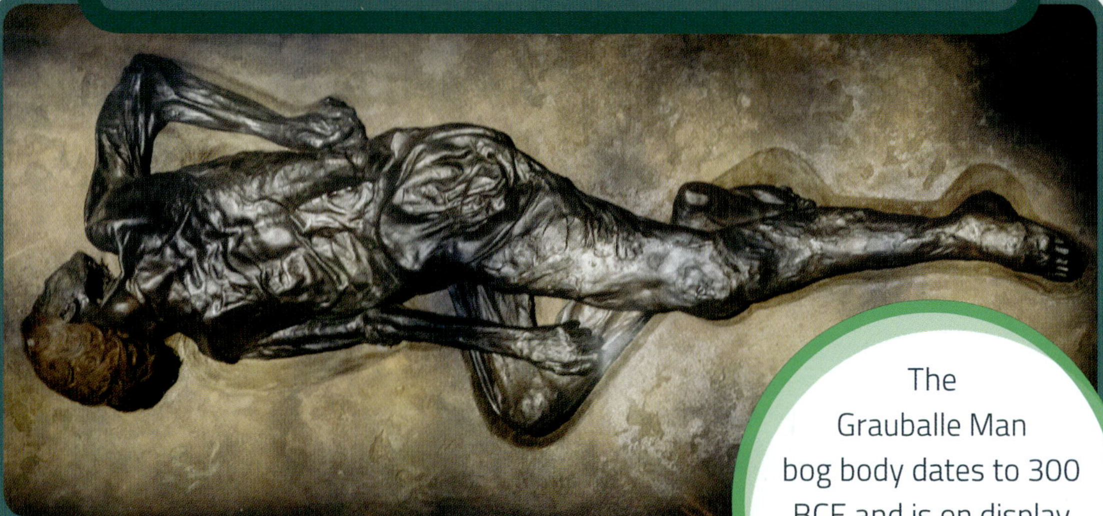

The Grauballe Man bog body dates to 300 BCE and is on display at the Moesgaard Museum in Denmark.

Peat bogs are a special type of wetland. They are acidic and don't have good oxygen content. Both of these conditions make it hard for microorganisms to survive. But it turns out they are ideal for mummifying bodies.

All over Northern Europe, archaeologists have found bog bodies. These are the remains of Bronze Age and Iron Age people. Some of them are almost perfectly preserved. They still have skin and organs. That's because there weren't any microorganisms like bacteria to eat them. Instead, the body was slowly preserved by the vinegar-like water. It is sort of like a cucumber turning into a pickle.

One of the most famous bog bodies is the Tollund Man. He was found in 1950 in Denmark. His facial features are easy to see. It almost looks like he is sleeping. Researchers have found porridge and seeds in his stomach.

The Tollund Man is a snapshot of Iron Age life in Denmark.

Researchers think he was a human sacrifice. He has a rope around his neck. They think he was hanged. But he was also placed carefully into the bog. His eyes and mouth are closed. He's positioned to look like he is sleeping. That leads researchers to think he was cared for after he died. The Tollund Man wasn't just tossed into the bog and left there.

4,000+

Age in years of the oldest known Bog Body

- The body was found in County Laois, Ireland, in 2011.
- Some researchers think he might have been a king who was sacrificed.
- Kings were sacrificed in Ireland at that time if people or livestock fell ill to a plague.

The bog body of Tollund Man dates to 375 to 210 BCE.

12 Wonders of the World Were Built

Three of what are known as the Seven Wonders of the Ancient World were built during the Iron Age.

The Hanging Gardens of Babylon were built between 605 and 562 BCE. No conclusive proof of their existence has ever been found. But ancient Greek and Roman texts paint pretty pictures. This was a large terraced structure. On each level of the terrace, different plants grew. The levels went as high as 75 feet (23 m). There were trees, flowers, and other plants. Imagine flowers cascading down walls and over steps. There were also waterfalls built in.

The Temple of Artemis was a large temple built for the Greek goddess of hunting and wild animals. It took 120 years

The Hanging Gardens of Babylon.

Ruins of the Temple of Artemis.

The tomb of Mausolus at Halicarnassus.

to build. Construction finished in 550 BCE. The temple was bigger than the Parthenon. It had 127 columns, each 60 feet (18 m) tall. For comparison, a street lamp is only about 25 feet (7.6 m) tall. This towering temple was burned to the ground in just one night by raiders.

The last Iron Age wonder was the Mausoleum at Halicarnassus. A mausoleum is a fancy grave. This one was built for a Persian satrap, or governor, named Mausolus. It was surrounded by ornate sculptures. Some of the sculptures that survive are life-size lions. Mausolus' tomb was so famous that's where the word "mausoleum" comes from.

THINK ABOUT IT

What would you include on a list of Seven Wonders of the Modern World? Give some reasons.

18

Years Stephanie Dalley spent researching the Hanging Gardens of Babylon

- Dalley, a British scholar, is an expert in ancient languages. She dug into old documents and translations.
- She believes the gardens weren't built in Babylon after all.
- Dalley thinks they were created at Nineveh, a city 300 miles away from Babylon.

Timeline of the Iron Age

The Iron Age lasted from around 3,200 years ago to 1,200 years ago.

3,200 years ago:
People start making iron weapons and tools.

2,632 years ago:
The Hanging Gardens of Babylon are built.

2,488 years ago:
The great Greek philosopher Socrates is born.

2,456 years ago:
The Parthenon is built in Athens.

2,350 years ago:
The Tollund Man is placed in a bog.

A viking sword from the Iron Age discovered in Norway.

2,343 years ago:
Alexander the Great starts conquering territories.

2,000 years ago:
Samhain is first celebrated by the Celts.

1,600 years ago:
The Roman Empire declines.

1,200 years ago:
The Vikings hit the scene.

Glossary

acidic
Something that contains acid; something that tastes sour or sharp.

barter
To negotiate a trade; to exchange things instead of money.

BCE
Before the Common Era. All the time leading up to the birth of Jesus of Nazareth. Years BCE are counted backward.

CE
The Common Era. All the time starting with the birth of Jesus of Nazareth and since then. Years CE are counted forward.

elegant
Beautiful or graceful.

groundwork
Something done at an early stage to prepare the way for something bigger.

manure
Fertilizer made of animal dung.

metalwork
Making something out of metal.

ore
Rock that contains a valuable metal, like iron, gold, or silver.

prehistoric
Before recorded history; from the time before people could write.

preserved
Kept in good condition; maintained close to its original form.

serve
To perform duties, as in the military or public office.

smelt
To get metal out of rock by melting it.

Read More

Bell, Samantha S. *Ancient Greece*. Civilizations of the World. Lake Elmo, MN: Focus Readers, 2020.

Bell, Samantha S. *Ancient Rome*. Civilizations of the World. Lake Elmo, MN: Focus Readers, 2020.

Samuels, Charles. *What Happened to Pompeii?* Mysteries in History: Solving the Mysteries of the Past. New York: Cavendish Square, 2017.

Index

About the Author
Meg Marquardt started out as a scientist but likes writing about science even more. She enjoys researching physics, geology, and climate science. She lives in Madison, Wisconsin, with her two scientist cats, Lagrange and Doppler.